T0401554

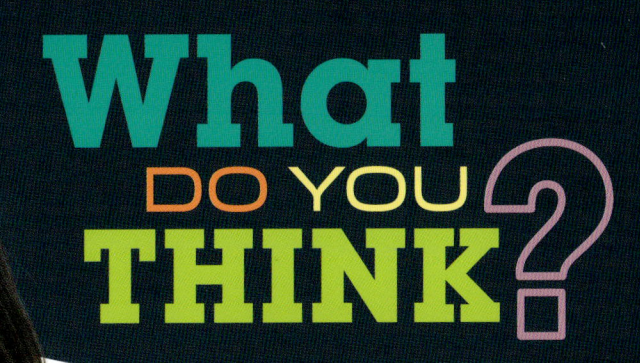

# What DO YOU THINK?

# SHOULD STUDENTS WEAR UNIFORMS?

BY RAYMIE DAVIS

Gareth Stevens
PUBLISHING

Please visit our website, www.garethstevens.com. For a free color catalog of all our high-quality books, call toll free 1-800-542-2595 or fax 1-877-542-2596.

**Library of Congress Cataloging-in-Publication Data**

Names: Davis, Raymie, author.
Title: Should students wear uniforms? / by Raymie Davis.
Description: New York : Gareth Stevens Publishing, 2023. | Series: What do you think? | Includes index. | Audience: Grades 2-3
Identifiers: LCCN 2021044970 (print) | LCCN 2021044971 (ebook) | ISBN 9781538278710 (paperback) | ISBN 9781538278734 (library binding) | ISBN 9781538278727 (set) | ISBN 9781538278741 (ebook)
Subjects: LCSH: Students–Uniforms–Juvenile literature. | Dress codes–Juvenile literature. | Students–Clothing–Juvenile literature.
Classification: LCC LB3024 .D38 2023 (print) | LCC LB3024 (ebook) | DDC 371.8–dc23/eng/20211012
LC record available at https://lccn.loc.gov/2021044970
LC ebook record available at https://lccn.loc.gov/2021044971

First Edition

Portions of this work were originally authored by Katie Kawa and published as *Are School Uniforms Good for Students?* All new material in this edition authored by Raymie Davis.

Published in 2023 by
**Gareth Stevens Publishing**
29 East 21st Street
New York, NY 10010

Copyright © 2023 Gareth Stevens Publishing

Editor: Caitie McAneney
Designer: Michael Flynn

Photo credits: Cover, p. 1 © triloks/iStock; back cover and series background MYMNY/Shutterstock.com; pp. 5, 7 (nurse) Monkey Business Images/Shutterstock.com; p. 7 (police officer) John Roman Images/Shutterstock.com; p. 7 (soldier) Lightfield Studios/Shutterstock.com; p. 7 (firefighter) Firefighter Montreal/Shutterstock.com; p. 9 4 PM production/Shutterstock.com; p. 11 wavebreakmedia/Shutterstock.com; pp. 12, 13 New Africa/Shutterstock.com; p. 15 Kiselev Andrey Valerevich/Shutterstock.com; p. 17 Sergey Ryzhov/Shutterstock.com; p. 19 Karpova/Shutterstock.com; p. 21 Roman Samborskyi/Shutterstock.com.

Printed in the United States of America

Some of the images in this book illustrate individuals who are models. The depictions do not imply actual situations or events.

CPSIA compliance information: Batch #CSGS23: For further information contact Gareth Stevens, New York, New York at 1-800-542-2595.

Find us on

# CONTENTS

WORDS IN THE GLOSSARY APPEAR IN **BOLD** TYPE THE FIRST TIME THEY ARE USED IN THE TEXT.

# UNIFORMS VS. CHOICE

It's time to get dressed for school. What do you wear? Some people choose something new to wear every day. They enjoy **expressing** themselves through clothing. But some students wear uniforms to school. They don't have much of a choice.

Uniforms are a set kind of clothing worn by every student at a school. Some people think uniforms are helpful. Other people think they are unnecessary. You can read both arguments to make an informed opinion of your own!

ARE SCHOOL UNIFORMS GOOD FOR STUDENTS? LOOK AT THE FACTS SO YOU CAN DECIDE FOR YOURSELF.

# WEARING UNIFORMS

Private schools, including **religious** schools, often require uniforms. Many public schools are also starting to make dress codes or uniform **policies**. These uniforms can include skirts or **jumpers**, certain kinds of pants or shorts, and shirts that must be a certain style or color. Some schools also require students to only wear certain kinds of socks and shoes.

Many jobs require people to wear uniforms. Police officers, nurses, firefighters, doctors, and airplane pilots are just some of the people who wear uniforms to work.

## Think ABOUT IT!

IN 2021, AROUND 20 PERCENT OF PUBLIC SCHOOLS IN THE UNITED STATES REQUIRED UNIFORMS.

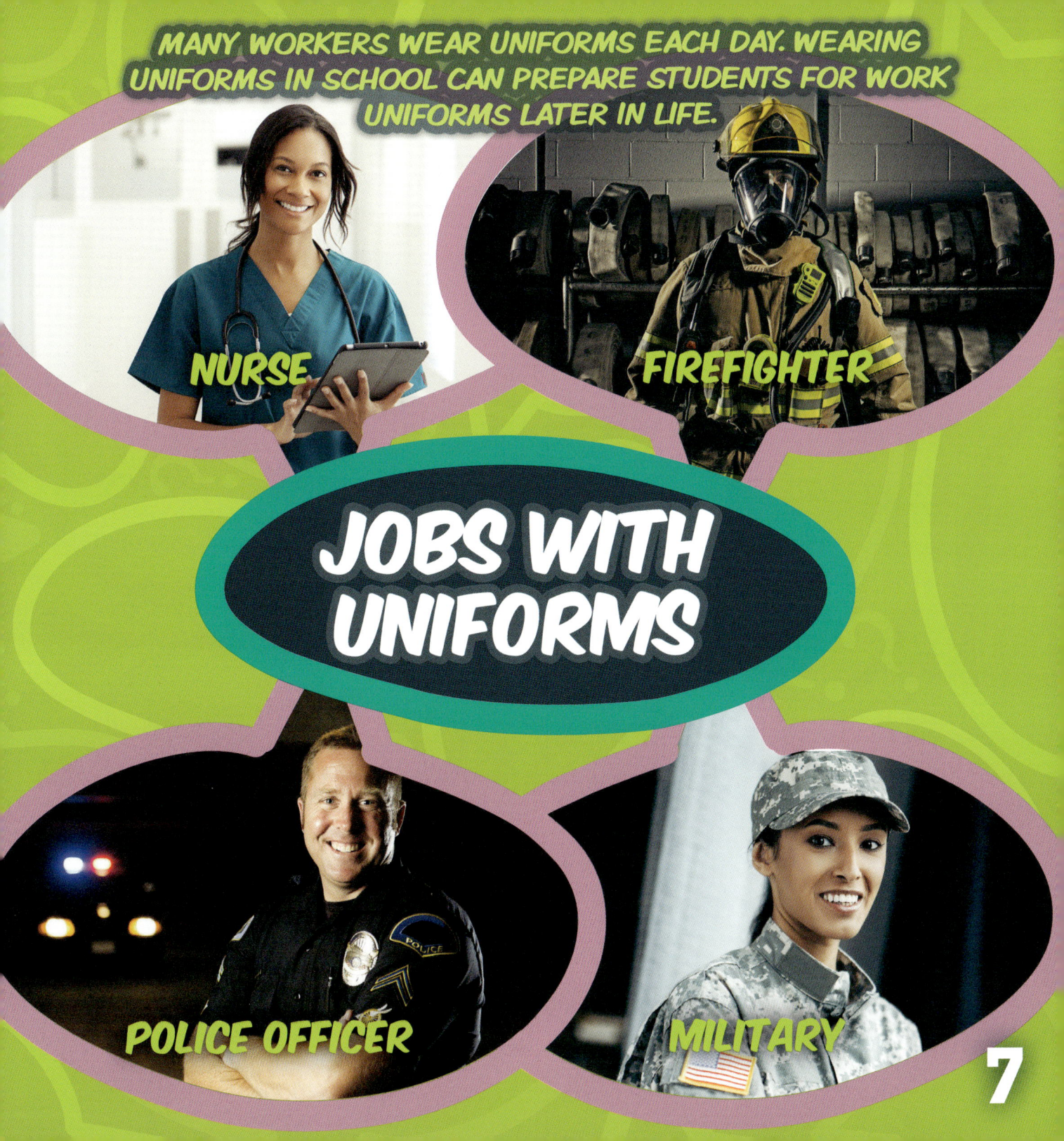

MANY WORKERS WEAR UNIFORMS EACH DAY. WEARING UNIFORMS IN SCHOOL CAN PREPARE STUDENTS FOR WORK UNIFORMS LATER IN LIFE.

NURSE

FIREFIGHTER

# JOBS WITH UNIFORMS

POLICE OFFICER

MILITARY

7

# PEER PRESSURE

Some people argue that allowing kids to choose clothing can make them feel **peer pressure** to dress a certain way. They might worry that their clothes aren't in style. They might be bullied for wearing something different.

People who support school uniforms believe this would happen less if students all had to dress the same. Uniforms can lower the chance that students will be bullied because of what they're wearing. Students wouldn't have to worry about wearing the latest fashion trend.

A 2018 BRIGHAM YOUNG UNIVERSITY STUDY FOUND THAT A MAJORITY OF OLDER STUDENTS REPORTED THAT SCHOOL UNIFORMS REDUCED BULLYING AT SCHOOL

UNIFORMS CAN TAKE THE PRESSURE OFF STUDENTS TO DRESS A CERTAIN WAY TO AVOID BULLYING OR TEASING.

# TARGETED BY BULLIES

Some people argue that uniform policies won't stop bullies from **targeting** someone. Bullies can still single out students for how they choose to wear their uniform. For example, a girl might be teased for wearing pants instead of a skirt, even if both are part of her school's uniform.

Some people argue that uniforms can actually make young people the targets of bullies from other schools that don't have uniforms. They might be bullied for wearing their school colors by kids at a **rival** school.

UNIFORMS MAY MAKE STUDENTS FIT IN WHILE THEY'RE IN SCHOOL—BUT THEY MIGHT STAND OUT IN THEIR NEIGHBORHOOD.

11

# LEARNING LIFE SKILLS

Following rules is important to keep things safe and fair. Rules are a part of everyday life—from the speed limits on the road to the rules in an office. Discipline, or the practice of following rules, is an important life skill.

Some people argue that wearing a uniform at school gives children a rule to follow every day from the time they're young. This **encourages** discipline in schools. Discipline can help students take their schoolwork more seriously.

PEOPLE ARGUE THAT UNIFORMS MAKE STUDENTS LOOK MORE **PROFESSIONAL.** THAT MIGHT MAKE STUDENTS ACT MORE PROFESSIONAL.

# EXPRESS YOURSELF!

Many people express themselves through art, music, and even clothing. What someone wears can tell their classmates what they care about or what their style is. They can also decide to dress comfortably.

Some people think school uniforms keep students from expressing themselves. They want students to feel free to be themselves. They also argue uniforms stop students from dressing in a way that honors different cultures, or ways of life. Clothing can celebrate **diversity**, while uniforms make everyone look the same.

CHOOSING YOUR OWN CLOTHING CAN HELP YOU FEEL COMFORTABLE AND CREATIVE.

15

# COSTLY CLOTHING

New clothes can cost a lot of money, especially if you want to wear something new each day. At the start of the school year, many families go back-to-school shopping, which often means buying many new clothes and spending a lot of money.

People only need to buy a few pieces of clothing for a school uniform instead of many new outfits to keep up with what other students are wearing. People can save money and time for back-to-school shopping when uniforms are required.

## Think ABOUT IT!

THE NATIONAL RETAIL FEDERATION SAID THAT IN 2019, FAMILIES WITH STUDENTS PLANNED TO SPEND AN AVERAGE OF $696.70 ON BACK-TO-SCHOOL SHOPPING.

WEARING A UNIFORM CAN LOWER THE AMOUNT OF MONEY SPENT ON CLOTHING DURING A SCHOOL YEAR.

17

# EXPENSIVE UNIFORMS

Some people argue that school uniforms can cost more money. Parents are required to buy specific pieces of clothing, which might be more costly than something they might have chosen otherwise.

If a school doesn't require a uniform, students can wear old clothing or cheaper clothing. Plus, they can buy clothing only when they need it. The basic parts of a uniform, however, must be bought all at once before a student can start school. That can be hard for families to afford.

# Think ABOUT IT!

SOME UNIFORMS CAN BE BOUGHT FROM REGULAR STORES. OTHERS ARE OFFICIAL UNIFORMS FROM A SPECIFIC SELLER, WHICH CAN BE EXPENSIVE.

SOME STUDENTS NEED TO WEAR SPECIAL BLAZERS, OR JACKETS, TO SCHOOL THESE ARE OFTEN EXPENSIVE.

# WHAT'S BEST FOR STUDENTS?

Adults who argue for and against uniforms have many different reasons. Some think uniforms are costly, while others say chosen clothing is more costly. Students often share their thoughts and experiences, too. Some students say uniforms aren't comfortable. Other students say uniforms cut down on the amount of time it takes to get ready.

You've seen the arguments and facts. Now you can use them to make an informed opinion. Do you think students should wear uniforms? What do you think is best for students?

WHAT'S YOUR EXPERIENCE WITH UNIFORMS? YOU CAN USE YOUR EXPERIENCE AS YOU MAKE YOUR ARGUMENT.

# GLOSSARY

**diversity:** the quality or state of having many different types, forms, or ideas

**encourage:** to make someone more likely to do something

**express:** to show a person's true self or creative abilities

**jumper:** a sleeveless dress often worn with a shirt under it

**peer pressure:** a feeling that one must do the same things as others to be liked by them

**policy:** a set of rules for how something is to be done

**professional:** done as if for a job, with great care

**religious:** relating to a system of beliefs, often belief in God, held with faith and strong feeling

**rival:** a person or group fighting against another person or group to win or succeed

**target:** a person someone aims an attack at

# FOR MORE INFORMATION

## BOOKS

Connors, Kathleen. *What's School Like Around the World?* New York, NY: Cavendish Square Publishing, 2022.

Jeffries, Corina. *Following Rules at School: Understanding Citizenship.* New York, NY: Rosen Classroom, 2019.

Owens, Layla. *Should Schools Have Dress Codes?* New York, NY: KidHaven Publishing, 2022.

## WEBSITES

**Are School Dress Codes Fair?**
*choices.scholastic.com/issues/2018-19/020119/are-school-dress-codes-fair.html*
Take a look at the arguments for and against school dress codes to make your own opinion.

**Dealing with Bullies**
*kidshealth.org/en/kids/bullies.html#catemotion*
Learn how to deal with bullies at school.

**Dealing with Peer Pressure**
*kidshealth.org/en/kids/peer-pressure.html#catemotion*
How can you deal with peer pressure at school? This resource gives you some ideas that you can apply to the school uniform debate.

# INDEX